I ♥ MY MOM

A mother is your first friend, your best friend, your forever friend.

Moms are the people
who know us the best
and love us the most.

A mother's love is the fuel that enables a normal human being to do the impossible

A mother's love is
the fuel that enables
a normal human
being to do the
impossible

A mother is she who can take the place of all others but whose place no one else can take.

There is nothing as powerful as mother's love, and nothing as healing as a child's soul.

I love my mother as trees love water and sunshine. She helps me grow, prosper, and reach great heights.

When you are a mother, you are never really alone in your thoughts. A mother always has to think twice, once for herself and once for her child.

Mother's love is peace. It need not be acquired; it need not be deserved.

My mother is the most beautiful woman I ever saw. All I am I owe to my mother. I attribute my success in life to the moral, intellectual and physical education I received from her.

A mother is not a person to lean on, but a person to make leaning unnecessary."

You're My One And Only Dad, And I'll Always Have A Special Place In My Heart For You.

To describe my mother would be to write about a hurricane in its perfect power. Or the climbing, falling colors of a rainbow.

Mama is my greatest teacher, a teacher of compassion, love and fearlessness. If love is sweet as a flower, then my mother is that sweet flower of love."